S0-DXL-245

Our Bearable World
– Featuring the Imagination Bears –

by
Joel Gresham

A fun way for children to learn
about the environment
and the world they live in.

Copyright 2005© by Joel Gresham
All rights reserved.
No part(s) of this book may be used or reproduced in any
manner whatsoever without prior written permission,
except in the context of reviews.

Library of Congress Cataloging-in-Publication Data

ISBN 0-970446-8-9

Special thanks and love to Destiny for all her wonderful support.

Our Bearable World
Featuring the Imagination Bears

Written by Joel Gresham
Created by Joel Gresham
Illustrations by Joel Gresham

Our Bearable World
Featuring the Imagination Bears

Summary: A fun way for children to learn about the environment and the world they live in.

Contact: Joel Gresham / Undercolorjg@yahoo.com

Dr. Beartree

Taking care of our earth
we all must do. If we take
care of her, she will take
care of you.

Airbear

Airbear thought . . . A revolution to wipe out air pollution. Wow! That's the perfect solution. Oh dear! Let me whisper something in your ear. Imagine a clear atmosphere!

Boxy Bear

At the Bear Box Factory here's what I see: recycled boxes counted to a tee. Box, blocks and lots of boxes! One, two, three . . . stacked to the ceiling as high as can be.

Envirobear

Fitting snug like his rubber gloves. A chemical suit in his boots, toxic gas and hazardous waste, he wears a mask to protect his face.

Ms. Bearable

Ms. Bearable thought how cool it is to pick up at your school . . . but then she thought, a great way to start is to pick up in your own backyard.

H2 the Obear
(can you rap this?)

H2 the O don't you know? Oceans and rivers we must keep aflow. Lakes, canals, creeks, and streams, let's form a party to keep them clean. Picking up trash along the banks. Animal waste that's a no thanks. Chemical, garbage, sewage and oil, that's enough pollution to make us boil. H2 the O don't you know? Oceans and rivers we must keep aflow.

(Repeat)

Recycle Bear

Plastic bottles, packaging, papers and cans, let's recycle these items, again and again.

Mr. Unbearable

Here's a silly character you've seen around. He's always throwing trash on the ground. His name is Unbearable and he lives in your town. You know when you've met him because of his frown.

Bearservation

With my binocular I can see that little bear behind a tree. Birds, butterflies, flowers and trees. I like looking at them on my knees.

Greeny Bear

Planting seeds, trees to breathe. Greenery will keep us in the scenery.

Recycle Scramble Words

1. dereuc

2. ceylcer

3. serue

recycle bear

Recycle Scramble Words

1. olsi

2. taewr

3. aofm

h2 the obear

Recycle Scramble Words

1. eman

2. tilert

3. esyms

mr. unbearable

Recycle Scramble Words

1. mwragni

2. uppl

3. etwndasl

envirobear

Recycle Scramble Words

1. velo

2. rcae

3. evsa

dr. beartree

Recycle Scramble Words

1. turaen

2. ase

3. diet

bearservation

Recycle Scramble Words

1. usn

2. rtdi

3. esdes

greeny bear

Recycle Scramble Words

1. etre

2. nerge

3. ogwr

boxy bear

Environment Journal

how can you stop water pollution?

Environment Journal

write about things to recycle.

Environment Journal

how can you stop air pollution?

Environment Journal

what can you do to keep the earth green?

Environment Journal

what can you do to conserve water?

Environment Journal

what can you do to conserve energy?

Environment Journal

where do you throw your trash?

Environment Journal

what do you do when you see trash on the ground?

Draw Your Own Envirobear!

Draw Your Own Envirobear!

Draw Your Own Envirobear!

Answers

reduce...recycle...reuse

soil...water...foam

sun...dirt...seeds

tree...green...grow

love...care...save

mean...litter...messy

nature...sea...tide

warming...pulp...wetlands

About the Artist / Author

Joel Gresham, artist, author, and inventor, was born in Fort Lauderdale, Florida. He received his art training at the Atlanta University Center. His remarkable gift as a painter and author has brought him significant acclaim. He has been featured in more than 21 solo exhibits, and 30 group exhibits. Joel's artwork has been used on TV for popular sitcoms, and he has received credit for artwork in books in addition to other special promotions. As a three dimensional artist he has crafted award-winning designs for corporate, music and television personalities. Joel has created *The Imagination Bears*, a new and exciting book and animation series for children.

His works are in many public and private collections including Oprah, Quincy Jones, Edwin Moses, Bernie Marcus, Rudolph Giuliani, Sam Massell, Robert Gillaume, Paul Winfield, Marla Gibbs, Hank Aaron, James Worthy, and Muhammad Ali.

"As an artist, I've discovered that maintaining strong fundamentals in my art allowed me to develop my own unique style. I capture symmetry and harmonic balance of line and movement, by reinforcing basic principles and communicating their close relationships to life."